Physicians: Money for Life

Action Guide

Dennis M. Postema

Module 1:
The Economic Problems Facing Today's Preretirees

If you could retire now, would you want to, as 60 percent of your peers said they would in a 2012 Physician's Foundation survey? If not now, what is your ideal retirement age?

_____

_____

_____

What's stopping you from retiring when you want?

_____

_____

_____

_____

Do you have a financial planner offering you safe, sane solutions to help you retire at your ideal age?

_____

_____

Planning for Unexpected Expenses

What are some "unexpected expenses" you need to be aware of in retirement? What do you think you'll need to prepare for in retirement? Consider all the hobbies you currently enjoy and activities you plan to take part in after retirement.

_____

_____

_____

_____

_____

_____

_____

How can you plan for these unexpected expenses?

_____

_____

_____

_____

Planning for Potential Dangers

There are many potential dangers in retirement. Describe how each of those listed below may affect you as well as how you can avoid them.

Market Turbulence

_____

_____

_____

_____

_____

Increased Cost of Living

_____

_____

_____

_____

_____

Increased Life Expectancy

_____

_____

_____

_____

_____

_____

Disappearing or Less-Dependable Sources of Income

_____

_____

_____

_____

_____

_____

Know Your Budget

An important step to take in entering retirement is to have your financial future in order. Fill in the blanks below to get a thorough understanding of your budget.

Write your estimated monthly retirement expenses below.

Mortgage/Rent Payments	
Association Dues or Condo Fees	
Property Taxes	
Utilities (power, phone, cable, etc.)	
Homeowner's Insurance	
Yearly Household Maintenance	
Groceries	
Dining Out	
Car Loan or Lease Payment	
Auto Insurance	
Gas	
Auto Maintenance (repairs, oil changes, etc.)	
Public Transportation (bus, train, subway, etc.)	
Health Insurance	
Medicare/Medigap and Other Premium Payments	
Prescription Medications	

Dental, Hearing or Vision	
Life Insurance	
Long-Term Care Insurance	
Disability Insurance	
Clothing	
Personal Care Expenses (haircuts, laundry, etc.)	
Gifts (holidays, events, birthdays, etc.)	
Charitable or Religious Donations	
Entertainment and Recreation	
Travel	
Hobby Expenses	
Education or Training	
Family Care (parents, children, grandchildren, etc.)	
Income Tax	
Other	
TOTAL (Equals your total monthly income needed)	

In the below boxes, write your estimated monthly retirement income streams.

Social Security	
Investments	
Salary or Wages from Employment	
Pension	
Annuity Income	
Rental Income	
Other	
TOTAL MONTHLY INCOME	

In the below boxes, write your <u>current</u> investment and savings vehicles.

Retirement Plan Accounts (401(k), 403(b), 457, TSP)

1. Name of Vehicle	
Name of Institution (Where are they held?)	
Total Asset Value ($)	
2. Name of Vehicle	
Name of Institution (Where are they held?)	
Total Asset Value ($)	
3. Name of Vehicle	
Name of Institution (Where are they held?)	
Total Asset Value ($)	

IRA Accounts (IRA, Simple IRA, Roth IRA, etc.)

1. Name of Vehicle	
Name of Institution (Where are they held?)	
Total Asset Value ($)	
2. Name of Vehicle	
Name of Institution (Where are they held?)	
Total Asset Value ($)	
3. Name of Vehicle	
Name of Institution (Where are they held?)	
Total Asset Value ($)	

Mutual Funds

1. Name of Vehicle	
Name of Institution (Where are they held?)	
Total Asset Value ($)	
2. Name of Vehicle	
Name of Institution (Where are they held?)	
Total Asset Value ($)	
3. Name of Vehicle	
Name of Institution (Where are they held?)	
Total Asset Value ($)	

Annuities

1. Name of Vehicle	
Name of Institution (Where are they held?)	
Total Asset Value ($)	
2. Name of Vehicle	
Name of Institution (Where are they held?)	
Total Asset Value ($)	
3. Name of Vehicle	
Name of Institution (Where are they held?)	
Total Asset Value ($)	

Life Insurance

1. Name of Vehicle	
Name of Institution (Where are they held?)	
Total Asset Value ($)	
2. Name of Vehicle	
Name of Institution (Where are they held?)	
Total Asset Value ($)	
3. Name of Vehicle	
Name of Institution (Where are they held?)	
Total Asset Value ($)	

Disability Insurance

1. Name of Vehicle	
Name of Institution (Where are they held?)	
Total Asset Value ($)	
2. Name of Vehicle	
Name of Institution (Where are they held?)	
Total Asset Value ($)	
3. Name of Vehicle	
Name of Institution (Where are they held?)	
Total Asset Value ($)	

Long-Term Care Insurance

1. Name of Vehicle	
Name of Institution (Where are they held?)	
Total Asset Value ($)	
2. Name of Vehicle	
Name of Institution (Where are they held?)	
Total Asset Value ($)	
3. Name of Vehicle	
Name of Institution (Where are they held?)	
Total Asset Value ($)	

Bank Accounts (Checking, Savings, CD, etc.)

1. Name of Vehicle	
Name of Institution (Where are they held?)	
Total Asset Value ($)	
2. Name of Vehicle	
Name of Institution (Where are they held?)	
Total Asset Value ($)	
3. Name of Vehicle	
Name of Institution (Where are they held?)	
Total Asset Value ($)	

In the below boxes, write your current liabilities.

Mortgage #1

Company Name	
Interest Rate	
Loan Balance	
Minimum Payment	

Mortgage #2

Company Name	
Interest Rate	
Loan Balance	
Minimum Payment	

Auto Loan #1

Company Name	
Interest Rate	
Loan Balance	
Minimum Payment	

Auto Loan #2

Company Name	
Interest Rate	
Loan Balance	
Minimum Payment	

Auto Loan #3

Company Name	
Interest Rate	
Loan Balance	
Minimum Payment	

Credit Card #1

Company Name	
Interest Rate	
Loan Balance	
Minimum Payment	

Credit Card #2

Company Name	
Interest Rate	
Loan Balance	
Minimum Payment	

Credit Card #3

Company Name	
Interest Rate	
Loan Balance	
Minimum Payment	

Credit Card #4

Company Name	
Interest Rate	
Loan Balance	
Minimum Payment	

Line of Credit

Company Name	
Interest Rate	
Loan Balance	
Minimum Payment	

Student Loan #1

Company Name	
Interest Rate	
Loan Balance	
Minimum Payment	

Student Loan #2

Company Name	
Interest Rate	
Loan Balance	
Minimum Payment	

Other #1

Company Name	
Interest Rate	
Loan Balance	
Minimum Payment	

Other #2

Company Name	
Interest Rate	
Loan Balance	
Minimum Payment	

Module 2:
Redefining Financial Planning Rules

The role of a financial planner: To help average people learn how to spend, save, invest, insure and plan wisely for the future to achieve financial independence.

What does each point of the financial planner's role mean to you?

Spend: _____

_____

_____

_____

_____

Save: _____

_____

_____

_____

_____

Invest: _____

_____

_____

_____

_____

Insure: _____

_____

_____

_____

_____

Plan: _____

_____

_____

_____

_____

How does your current financial plan incorporate each of these points?

_____

_____

_____

_____

_____

_____

_____

Does your current financial plan promote financial independence? If so, how?

_____

_____

_____

_____

_____

If not, what changes could you make so it does?

_____

_____

_____

_____

_____

In your investing lifetime, have you personally felt the effects of a stock market downturn? If so, think back on that time and describe how you felt watching your assets lose value.

_____

_____

_____

_____

_____

_____

_____

Accumulation versus Preservation

What steps are you currently taking to accumulate more wealth?

_____

_____

_____

_____

What steps are you taking to preserve your wealth?

_____

_____

_____

_____

Are you focusing more on accumulation than preservation?

_____

_____

_____

_____

If so, what steps can you take to bring your focus back to preservation?

_____

_____

_____

_____

_____

Points of Consideration

In the book, you were asked to consider several points about your current financial situation and approach to saving/investing. Now, let's address each of those points.

Are you okay risking everything in order to have the potential for a higher return?

_____

_____

Do you have enough in CDs and other fixed investments that, if they have low returns that don't keep up with inflation, you will not run out of money?

_____

_____

_____

How will you feel if you put all your money into the market and lose 50 percent?

_____

_____

_____

_____

How would you feel if you put your money into something more secure and made only 8 percent when the market has risen 10 percent?

_____

_____

_____

_____

Which of the last two scenarios hurts worse?

_____

_____

_____

What is more important to you at this phase of your life: accumulating more dollars or preserving what you've saved?

_____

_____

_____

_____

_____

How much does control mean to you? Is it more important for you to be able to choose each individual investment you have or to find a means of guaranteeing a postretirement income? Why?

_____

_____

_____

_____

_____

_____

_____

Module 3:
Retirement Planning Challenges

How Risky Is Your Portfolio?

To which of the following risks are your current retirement accounts exposed?

Interest rate risk: the risk that you'll get locked into a noncompetitive interest rate

Inflation risk: the risk that the fixed interest rate won't keep pace with inflation

Reinvestment risk: the risk that earnings and principal won't be reinvested at a comparable rate after maturity

Market risk: a risk of loss brought on by movement in the stock market

Retirement Plan Accounts (401(k), 403(b), 457, TSP)

1. Name of Vehicle	
Name of Institution (Where are they held?)	
Total Asset Value ($)	
2. Name of Vehicle	
Name of Institution (Where are they held?)	
Total Asset Value ($)	
3. Name of Vehicle	
Name of Institution (Where are they held?)	
Total Asset Value ($)	

IRA Accounts (IRA, Simple IRA, Roth IRA, etc.)

1. Name of Vehicle	
Name of Institution (Where are they held?)	
Total Asset Value ($)	
2. Name of Vehicle	
Name of Institution (Where are they held?)	
Total Asset Value ($)	
3. Name of Vehicle	
Name of Institution (Where are they held?)	
Total Asset Value ($)	

Mutual Funds

1. Name of Vehicle	
Name of Institution (Where are they held?)	
Total Asset Value ($)	
2. Name of Vehicle	
Name of Institution (Where are they held?)	
Total Asset Value ($)	
3. Name of Vehicle	
Name of Institution (Where are they held?)	
Total Asset Value ($)	

Annuities

1. Name of Vehicle	
Name of Institution (Where are they held?)	
Total Asset Value ($)	
2. Name of Vehicle	
Name of Institution (Where are they held?)	
Total Asset Value ($)	
3. Name of Vehicle	
Name of Institution (Where are they held?)	
Total Asset Value ($)	

Bank Accounts (Checking, Savings, CD, etc.)

1. Name of Vehicle	
Name of Institution (Where are they held?)	
Total Asset Value ($)	
2. Name of Vehicle	
Name of Institution (Where are they held?)	
Total Asset Value ($)	
3. Name of Vehicle	
Name of Institution (Where are they held?)	
Total Asset Value ($)	

Do you see any similar or worrying themes and trends in the risks you just identified?

_____

_____

_____

_____

_____

What can you do to change your risk exposure and protect yourself against these risks?

_____

_____

_____

_____

_____

Module 4:
Better Retirement Planning with Annuities

Annuities: Contractual accounts issued by life insurance companies that protect against the risk of outliving your retirement savings.

It's important to know and understand the differences between single premiums and flexible premiums. In the space below, note those differences as well as pros and cons of each.

Single Premium	Flexible Premium

Which annuity do you believe works best for you? Why?

_____

_____

_____

_____

_____

Know Your Annuities

In the spaces below, take notes on each listed annuity. What are the benefits of each? Who needs this type of annuity? What should you be aware of?

Fixed Annuity

_____

_____

_____

_____

_____

_____

Multi-Year Guarantee Annuity

_____

_____

_____

_____

_____

_____

Variable Annuity

_____

_____

_____

_____

_____

Indexed Annuity

_____

_____

_____

_____

_____

_____

Immediate Annuity

_____

_____

_____

_____

_____

Annuity Riders: When added to an annuity, a rider becomes a contractual obligation, which usually creates an added cost to the annuity. It puts a little less of your principal to work for you.

Take notes on of the following riders, why they are important and what you might want for yourself in retirement.

Cost of Living Adjustment Rider

_____

_____

_____

_____

Guaranteed Minimum Accumulation Benefit Rider

_____

_____

_____

_____

Guaranteed Minimum Income Benefit Rider

_____

_____

_____

_____

Terminal Illness Rider

_____

_____

_____

_____

_____

Long-Term Care Rider

_____

_____

_____

_____

_____

What's the best benefit rider for you? Why?

_____

_____

_____

_____

_____

Module 5:
Indexed Annuities

Indexed Annuity: A savings contract that allows you to invest your principal and allows it to grow based on the performance of any chosen subaccount, which is modeled to perform like a stock index, such as the NASDAQ, S&P 500, or Dow Jones Industrial Average.

What are some benefits you can experience through an indexed annuity? What would that change for you and your retirement?

_____

_____

_____

_____

What is the benefit trifecta that accompanies indexed annuities?

1. _____

_____

2. _____

_____

3. _____

_____

Accumulation

How can being cautious and conservative help you in the accumulation phase?

_____

_____

_____

_____

How can being cautious and conservative hurt you in the accumulation phase? How will you know when to take risks?

_____

_____

_____

_____

What are some tax benefits you can experience from indexed annuities? How can _you_ take advantage of these benefits?

_____

_____

_____

_____

What are the benefits of diversification in your annuities?

_____

_____

_____

_____

Distribution

In the space below, list the differences between distribution and preservation.

Distribution	Preservation

Which phase are you in right now? Why?

_____

_____

_____

_____

Which phase *should* you be in? Why?

_____

_____

_____

_____

How can you focus your mindset on the phase you may be in or the one you need to be in?

_____

_____

_____

_____

What is your financial goal for the future? Is it to leave a legacy for your heirs? To set up a healthy retirement for yourself? To give back to the community? What do you most want to accomplish?

_____

_____

_____

_____

_____

Based on that answer, what do you think is the best financial decision for you? Is life insurance a more valuable option for you? Why or why not?

_____

_____

_____

_____

Module 6:
Guaranteed Income Benefits

What are the key benefits of the GIB rider?

_____

_____

_____

_____

The Four Points of Power

Take notes on each of the GIB Four Points of Power below.

1. There Are No Downside Risks

_____

_____

_____

_____

_____

2. Guaranteed Income for Life

_____

_____

_____

_____

3. Income and Growth Flexibility

_____

_____

_____

_____

4. Control

_____

_____

_____

_____

What fees do you need to be aware of before investing in an indexed annuity? Ask your advisor to walk through these, and take notes from the information your advisor shares as well as from that provided in the book.

_____

_____

_____

_____

_____

_____

_____

_____

State Guaranty Associations

What are the maximum guaranty funds for your state? What role does this play in your annuity?

_____

_____

_____

Based on your answers from this module, what decision do you feel is best for you and your retirement? What will reap the best benefits and why?

_____

_____

_____

_____

_____

_____

_____

_____

_____

_____

_____

_____

Module 7:
Achieving Your Retirement Dreams

Know Your Vision

How do you envision your retirement? Do you want to live on the beach? Do you want to live in a larger home? What do you want your lifestyle to be? Describe your ideal retirement lifestyle, in detail, in the space below.

_____

_____

_____

_____

_____

_____

_____

_____

_____

_____

Know Your Goals

What retirement goals do you need to achieve in order to live the lifestyle vision you just outlined on the previous page? Write at least five specific goals and make a timeframe in which you want to achieve them.

1. _____

_____

2. _____

_____

3. _____

_____

4. _____

_____

5. _____

_____

**Review your budget worksheets from Module 1 and answers from all the modules. Then, go to the worksheet on the following page, and fill in the amounts you WANT to make versus the amounts you ARE making. Keep the goals you listed in mind as you do this exercise.

Expenses

Housing Expenses	Needs	Wants	Health Care Expenses	Needs	Wants
Mortgage/Rent	$	$	Heath Insurance Premiums	$	$
Home Insurance	$	$	Prescriptions	$	$
Real Estate Taxes	$	$	Co-pays/Co-Insurance	$	$
Utilities	$	$	Long Term Care Insurance	$	$
Other	$	$	**Living Expenses**		
Living Expenses			Taxes	$	$
Groceries	$	$	Life Insurance Premiums	$	$
Clothing	$	$	Charitable Contributions	$	$
Auto Payments	$	$	Recreation (hobbies, dining out, etc.)	$	$
Auto Insurance	$	$	Gifts to Family & Others	$	$
Additional Car Expenses (gas, registration, etc.)	$	$	Other	$	$
Travel	$	$		$	$
Other Living Expenses (home improvements, pets)	$	$			
A) Total Monthly Expenses (Needs + Wants)				$	

Income

Income Sources	Estimated Monthly Income
Pension Plan	$
Social Security	$
Investments	$
Part-time Employment	$
Other	$
B) Estimated Monthly Income	$

Compare your total monthly expenses to your potential sources of retirement income to identify potential gaps in your retirement income.

Total Monthly Expenses (A)	$
Total Estimated Monthly Income (B)	$
Monthly Retirement Income Gap (A-B)	$

Client Initials	Client Initials

2

Finding a Financial Representative

Now that you have defined your retirement budget and goals as well as gained an understanding of the different options available, the next step is to find a financial advisor.

Make a list of questions you want to ask a potential financial representative to ensure they are qualified for the job.

_____

_____

_____

_____

_____

What are some obvious warning signs that a financial representative may not be the best fit for you?

_____

_____

_____

_____

ADDITIONAL BOOKS AND PROGRAMS BY DENNIS M. POSTEMA

DESIGNING YOUR LIFE

What would happen if you discovered you could do more than just live your life—you could *design* it? This book teaches you to harness the power of your subconscious and program it to help you live a happy life fitting your definition of perfection.

DESIGNING YOUR LIFE: ACTION GUIDE

These exercises help you master your subconscious, abolish negativity and raise self-esteem. This guide focuses on creative visualization and powerful affirmations, to control your life's design and master your future.

DEVELOPING PERSEVERANCE

A combination of internal roadblocks are holding you back, preventing you from persevering. This book shows you how to break through these self-imposed obstacles to begin moving along your true path, taking you further than you ever thought possible.

DEVELOPING PERSEVERANCE: ACTION GUIDE

With this guide, you'll learn about the unique roadblocks you've designed for yourself and explore the thoughts, feelings and events that impact your ability to succeed.

YOU DESERVE TO BE RICH

If you're busy blaming your lack of wealth on upbringing, education and environment, you're missing out on learning how easy it is to get rich. This book teaches you to throw away the excuses and focus on the 12 steps to securing a future of financial success.

YOU DESERVE TO BE RICH: ACTION GUIDE

You deserve an ideal life. This workbook helps you get there by providing activities and strategies that explain the rules of greatness, help define your dreams and work to banish your fears.

UNLEASH YOUR MOJO

You already possess everything you need to be the person you want to be, you just have to access these powerful traits. In *Unleash Your Mojo*, you'll learn to recognize all the greatness inside you and discover how to put it to use and start living your ideal life.

UNLEASH YOUR MOJO: ACTION GUIDE

Each of us has power to succeed yet many of us never tap into that power. Instead we stagnate on the sidelines while others flash forward in life. This workbook gives practical tips, advice and exercises to advance in your quest for authenticity and power.

THE POSITIVE EDGE

There's a secret behind living a happy, successful, fulfilling life: *Positivity*. Learn how to overcome your tendency toward negativity, how to control your life and future, and how easy it is to improve your confidence and self-esteem.

SPARK: THE KEY TO IGNITING RADICAL CHANGE IN YOUR BUSINESS

A complete, step-by-step training program to help you become a high-performer and higher earner. Learn how to rise to the top of your profession, position yourself as an expert and attract the abundance you desire.

DARE TO SUCCEED

Get the motivation and the information you need to rise to the next level of success! America's #1 Success Coach, Jack Canfield, has gathered together the top business minds in one powerful book. This guide contains their secret strategies to conquer the competition and bring ongoing abundance into your life.

VICTORY JOURNAL

The *Victory Journal* demonstrates the importance of writing down all your daily wins. Inside you'll find exercises to help define your ideal self and create action steps to move closer to your goals.

HARNESSING THE POWER OF GRATITUDE

Recognize the positive energy moving through your day and harness it with this undated journal. Filled with inspirational quotes to help you maintain the spirit of gratitude, it's an ideal tool for developing an enduring, powerful habit of thankfulness.

APPRECIATING ALL THAT YOU HAVE

This 365-day journal filled with inspirational quotes provides a safe space to write down the many things you're thankful for. It's the perfect way to help shift your perspective and recognize the abundance of positive forces in your life.

THE PSYCHOLOGY OF SALES: FROM AVERAGE TO RAINMAKER

Take your sales from lackluster to rainmaker without any smarm, aggressive tactics or dishonesty. This book teaches sales pros the psychology of their customers so they can present products the right way for each shopper.

THE PSYCHOLOGY OF SALES: ACTION GUIDE

In this action guide, you'll gain greater insight into your own personality and psychological makeup as well as that of your customers so you can further your sales success and transform your career.

RETIREMENT YOU CAN'T OUTLIVE

Cut through the hype and challenge conventional wisdom with a book focusing on conservative and reasonable ways to save for retirement. This book uses plain language and lots of common sense that's been missing from financial planning sessions for decades.

RETIREMENT YOU CAN'T OUTLIVE: ACTION GUIDE

Transform the lessons taught in *Retirement You Can't Outlive* into action steps that change the shape of your financial future. This immersive tool contains worksheets, exercises and review sheets to help you develop a plan to rescue your financial future.

NAVIGATING THROUGH MEDICARE

Don't be confused by the rules, plans and parts of Medicare. This book simplifies the complex system and allows you to quickly and easily make the right decision for the future of your healthcare. It's a one-stop guide to everything you need to know.

AVOIDING A LEGACY NIGHTMARE

Poor planning can rip your estate from your loved ones. *Avoiding a Legacy Nightmare* is a simple guide to help you get started in creating an effective estate plan that achieves all that you intended.

PHYSICIANS: MONEY FOR LIFE

If you want to retire on your own terms, you must understand the special considerations that physicians need to make in order to maintain sustainable retirement plans. *Physicians: Money for Life* casts aside traditional advice that's not suited to conservative retirement planning and focuses on helping physicians design a plan that creates money for life.

PHYSICIANS: MONEY FOR LIFE: ACTION GUIDE

You have the knowledge necessary to change the financial health of your retirement, now it's time to apply it. This action guide helps you transform the lessons taught in *Physicians: Money for Life* into action steps you can take to change the shape of your retirement. With worksheets, exercises and review, this guide will help you move forward in your retirement planning journey while devising a plan to save it.

ALZHEIMER'S LEGACY GUIDE

Alzheimer's patients and their caregivers face a race against the clock and must learn how to cement a well-thought-out legacy plan before the disease's mental, emotional and psychological effects start to take their toll. This book provides guidance to both the recently diagnosed and those who will care for them as the disease progresses.

FINANCING YOUR LIFE: THE STORY OF FOUR FAMILIES

This is the story of four families that took their financial lives out of the red and into the black. There's McKenna, a single mom of two boys, working hard every day as a waitress; Toby and Shannon, two professionals battling a layoff and personal spending demons; Blake and Christine, a newlywed couple in a hurry to start living the good life, whether they can afford it or not; and Marcie and Kurt, two young parents struggling to keep up in an increasingly image-obsessed society.

FINANCING YOUR LIFE: THE FINANCIAL RECOVERY KIT

Financing Your Life is an innovative financial recovery kit devoted to teaching you how to take total control over your financial life. Within, you'll learn about the secret behind financial planning, budgeting basics, insurance, credit repair, getting out of debt, developing financial compromise with a spouse or partner, saving and investing, mortgages and more. This tool does more than just tell you about financial concepts; it helps you immediately begin integrating what you learn into your own financial life.

www.ingramcontent.com/pod-product-compliance
Lightning Source LLC
Chambersburg PA
CBHW081903170526
45167CB00007B/3129